THIS BOOK BELONGS TO

_____

ORDER OF CONTENTS

HOME DETAILS

HOUSEHOLD BILLS

MAJOR APPLIANCES

KITCHEN

LIVING ROOM

DINING ROOM

MASTER BEDROOM

BEDROOM 2

BEDROOM 3

BEDROOM 4

BEDROOM 5

BATHROOM 1

BATHROOM 2

BATHROOM 3

BATHROOM 4

ENTRANCE / HALLWAY

GARDEN

CUSTOM ROOMS

HOME DETAILS

ADDRESS	
YEAR HOUSE WAS BUILT	
PURCHASE DATE	
PURCHASE PRICE	
MORTGAGE PROVIDER	
OTHER DETAILS	

HOUSEHOLD BILLS

COST PER MONTH

BILL	PROVIDER	YEAR 1	YEAR 2	YEAR 3

MAJOR APPLIANCES

	ON MOVING IN
BRAND	
SUPPLIED BY	
DATE PURCHASED	
COST	
MODEL / SERIAL	
WARRANTY	
DIMENSIONS	
	REPLACEMENT
BRAND	
SUPPLIED BY	
DATE PURCHASED	
COST	
MODEL / SERIAL	
WARRANTY	
DIMENSIONS	

MAJOR APPLIANCES

	ON MOVING IN
BRAND	
SUPPLIED BY	
DATE PURCHASED	
COST	
MODEL / SERIAL	
WARRANTY	
DIMENSIONS	
	REPLACEMENT
BRAND	
SUPPLIED BY	
DATE PURCHASED	
COST	
MODEL / SERIAL	
WARRANTY	
DIMENSIONS	

MAJOR APPLIANCES

	ON MOVING IN
BRAND	
SUPPLIED BY	
DATE PURCHASED	
COST	
MODEL / SERIAL	
WARRANTY	
DIMENSIONS	
	REPLACEMENT
BRAND	
SUPPLIED BY	
DATE PURCHASED	
COST	
MODEL / SERIAL	
WARRANTY	
DIMENSIONS	

MAJOR APPLIANCES

	ON MOVING IN
BRAND	
SUPPLIED BY	
DATE PURCHASED	
COST	
MODEL / SERIAL	
WARRANTY	
DIMENSIONS	
	REPLACEMENT
BRAND	
SUPPLIED BY	
DATE PURCHASED	
COST	
MODEL / SERIAL	
WARRANTY	
DIMENSIONS	

MAJOR APPLIANCES

	ON MOVING IN
BRAND	
SUPPLIED BY	
DATE PURCHASED	
COST	
MODEL / SERIAL	
WARRANTY	
DIMENSIONS	
	REPLACEMENT
BRAND	
SUPPLIED BY	
DATE PURCHASED	
COST	
MODEL / SERIAL	
WARRANTY	
DIMENSIONS	

MAJOR APPLIANCES

	ON MOVING IN
BRAND	
SUPPLIED BY	
DATE PURCHASED	
COST	
MODEL / SERIAL	
WARRANTY	
DIMENSIONS	
	REPLACEMENT
BRAND	
SUPPLIED BY	
DATE PURCHASED	
COST	
MODEL / SERIAL	
WARRANTY	
DIMENSIONS	

MAJOR APPLIANCES

	ON MOVING IN
BRAND	
SUPPLIED BY	
DATE PURCHASED	
COST	
MODEL / SERIAL	
WARRANTY	
DIMENSIONS	
	REPLACEMENT
BRAND	
SUPPLIED BY	
DATE PURCHASED	
COST	
MODEL / SERIAL	
WARRANTY	
DIMENSIONS	

INTERIOR DESIGN PLAN

KITCHEN

DIMENSIONS _____

OF WINDOWS _____ # OF DOORS _____

WINDOW 1 SIZE _____ DOOR 1 _____

WINDOW 2 SIZE _____ DOOR 2 _____

WINDOW 3 SIZE _____ DOOR 3 _____

COLOR / STYLE _____

    WALLS _____

    FLOOR _____

    CEILING _____

    TRIM _____

    DOORS _____

NOTES / IDEAS

KITCHEN LAYOUT PLAN

KITCHEN TO DO LIST

TASK	FINISHED

KITCHEN QUOTES

DATE	COMPANY	SERVICE/JOB	PRICE	THOUGHTS

PURCHASED KITCHEN ITEMS

ITEM	SUPPLIER	COST
	TOTAL	

NOTES

INTERIOR DESIGN PLAN
LIVING ROOM

DIMENSIONS   _____

\# OF WINDOWS   _____   \# OF DOORS   _____

WINDOW 1 SIZE   _____   DOOR 1   _____

WINDOW 2 SIZE   _____   DOOR 2   _____

WINDOW 3 SIZE   _____   DOOR 3   _____

COLOR / STYLE   _____

     WALLS   _____

     FLOOR   _____

     CEILING   _____

     TRIM   _____

     DOORS   _____

NOTES / IDEAS

LIVING ROOM PLAN

LIVING ROOM TO DO LIST

TASK	FINISHED

LIVING ROOM QUOTES

DATE	COMPANY	SERVICE/JOB	PRICE	THOUGHTS

PURCHASED LIVING ROOM ITEMS

ITEM	SUPPLIER	COST
	TOTAL	

NOTES

INTERIOR DESIGN PLAN

DINING ROOM

DIMENSIONS _____

OF WINDOWS _____ # OF DOORS _____

WINDOW 1 SIZE _____ DOOR 1 _____

WINDOW 2 SIZE _____ DOOR 2 _____

WINDOW 3 SIZE _____ DOOR 3 _____

COLOR / STYLE _____

   WALLS _____

   FLOOR _____

   CEILING _____

   TRIM _____

   DOORS _____

NOTES / IDEAS

DINING ROOM PLAN

DINING ROOM TO DO LIST

TASK	FINISHED

DINING ROOM QUOTES

DATE	COMPANY	SERVICE/JOB	PRICE	THOUGHTS

PURCHASED DINING ROOM ITEMS

ITEM	SUPPLIER	COST
	TOTAL	

NOTES

_____

_____

_____

_____

_____

_____

_____

_____

_____

_____

_____

_____

_____

_____

_____

_____

_____

_____

_____

_____

_____

INTERIOR DESIGN PLAN
MASTER BEDROOM

DIMENSIONS _____

OF WINDOWS _____ # OF DOORS _____

WINDOW 1 SIZE _____ DOOR 1 _____

WINDOW 2 SIZE _____ DOOR 2 _____

WINDOW 3 SIZE _____ DOOR 3 _____

COLOR / STYLE _____

    WALLS _____

    FLOOR _____

    CEILING _____

    TRIM _____

    DOORS _____

NOTES / IDEAS

MASTER BEDROOM PLAN

MASTER BEDROOM TO DO LIST

TASK	FINISHED

MASTER BEDROOM QUOTES

DATE	COMPANY	SERVICE/JOB	PRICE	THOUGHTS

PURCHASED MASTER BEDROOM ITEMS

ITEM	SUPPLIER	COST
	TOTAL	

NOTES

INTERIOR DESIGN PLAN

BEDROOM 2

DIMENSIONS _____

OF WINDOWS _____ # OF DOORS _____

WINDOW 1 SIZE _____ DOOR 1 _____

WINDOW 2 SIZE _____ DOOR 2 _____

WINDOW 3 SIZE _____ DOOR 3 _____

COLOR / STYLE _____

    WALLS _____

    FLOOR _____

    CEILING _____

    TRIM _____

    DOORS _____

NOTES / IDEAS

BEDROOM 2 PLAN

BEDROOM 2 TO DO LIST

TASK	FINISHED

BEDROOM 2 QUOTES

DATE	COMPANY	SERVICE/JOB	PRICE	THOUGHTS

PURCHASED BEDROOM 2 ITEMS

ITEM	SUPPLIER	COST
	TOTAL	

NOTES

INTERIOR DESIGN PLAN

BEDROOM 3

DIMENSIONS _____

OF WINDOWS _____ # OF DOORS _____

WINDOW 1 SIZE _____ DOOR 1 _____

WINDOW 2 SIZE _____ DOOR 2 _____

WINDOW 3 SIZE _____ DOOR 3 _____

COLOR / STYLE _____

    WALLS _____

    FLOOR _____

    CEILING _____

    TRIM _____

    DOORS _____

NOTES / IDEAS

BEDROOM 3 PLAN

BEDROOM 3 TO DO LIST

TASK	FINISHED

BEDROOM 3 QUOTES

DATE	COMPANY	SERVICE/JOB	PRICE	THOUGHTS

PURCHASED BEDROOM 3 ITEMS

ITEM	SUPPLIER	COST
	TOTAL	

NOTES

INTERIOR DESIGN PLAN

BEDROOM 4

DIMENSIONS _____

OF WINDOWS _____ # OF DOORS _____

WINDOW 1 SIZE _____ DOOR 1 _____

WINDOW 2 SIZE _____ DOOR 2 _____

WINDOW 3 SIZE _____ DOOR 3 _____

COLOR / STYLE _____

   WALLS _____

   FLOOR _____

   CEILING _____

   TRIM _____

   DOORS _____

NOTES / IDEAS

BEDROOM 4 PLAN

BEDROOM 4 TO DO LIST

TASK	FINISHED

BEDROOM 4 QUOTES

DATE	COMPANY	SERVICE/JOB	PRICE	THOUGHTS

PURCHASED BEDROOM 4 ITEMS

ITEM	SUPPLIER	COST
	TOTAL	

NOTES

INTERIOR DESIGN PLAN

BEDROOM 5

DIMENSIONS _____

OF WINDOWS _____ # OF DOORS _____

WINDOW 1 SIZE _____ DOOR 1 _____

WINDOW 2 SIZE _____ DOOR 2 _____

WINDOW 3 SIZE _____ DOOR 3 _____

COLOR / STYLE _____

    WALLS _____

    FLOOR _____

    CEILING _____

    TRIM _____

    DOORS _____

NOTES / IDEAS

BEDROOM 5 PLAN

BEDROOM 5 TO DO LIST

TASK	FINISHED

BEDROOM 5 QUOTES

DATE	COMPANY	SERVICE/JOB	PRICE	THOUGHTS

PURCHASED BEDROOM 5 ITEMS

ITEM	SUPPLIER	COST
	TOTAL	

NOTES

_____

_____

_____

_____

_____

_____

_____

_____

_____

_____

_____

_____

_____

_____

_____

_____

_____

_____

_____

_____

_____

INTERIOR DESIGN PLAN

BATHROOM I

DIMENSIONS   _____

\# OF WINDOWS   _____   \# OF DOORS   _____

WINDOW 1 SIZE   _____   DOOR 1   _____

WINDOW 2 SIZE   _____   DOOR 2   _____

WINDOW 3 SIZE   _____   DOOR 3   _____

COLOR / STYLE   _____

   WALLS   _____

   FLOOR   _____

   CEILING   _____

   TRIM   _____

   DOORS   _____

NOTES / IDEAS

BATHROOM I PLAN

BATHROOM 1 TO DO LIST

TASK	FINISHED

BATHROOM | QUOTES

DATE	COMPANY	SERVICE/JOB	PRICE	THOUGHTS

PURCHASED BATHROOM I ITEMS

ITEM	SUPPLIER	COST
	TOTAL	

NOTES

INTERIOR DESIGN PLAN

BATHROOM 2

DIMENSIONS _____

OF WINDOWS _____ # OF DOORS _____

WINDOW 1 SIZE _____ DOOR 1 _____

WINDOW 2 SIZE _____ DOOR 2 _____

WINDOW 3 SIZE _____ DOOR 3 _____

COLOR / STYLE _____

    WALLS _____

    FLOOR _____

    CEILING _____

    TRIM _____

    DOORS _____

NOTES / IDEAS

BATHROOM 2 PLAN

BATHROOM 2 TO DO LIST

TASK	FINISHED

BATHROOM 2 QUOTES

DATE	COMPANY	SERVICE/JOB	PRICE	THOUGHTS

PURCHASED BATHROOM 2 ITEMS

ITEM	SUPPLIER	COST
	TOTAL	

NOTES

INTERIOR DESIGN PLAN

BATHROOM 3

DIMENSIONS _____

OF WINDOWS _____ # OF DOORS _____

WINDOW 1 SIZE _____ DOOR 1 _____

WINDOW 2 SIZE _____ DOOR 2 _____

WINDOW 3 SIZE _____ DOOR 3 _____

COLOR / STYLE _____

    WALLS _____

    FLOOR _____

    CEILING _____

    TRIM _____

    DOORS _____

NOTES / IDEAS

BATHROOM 3 PLAN

BATHROOM 3 TO DO LIST

TASK	FINISHED

BATHROOM 3 QUOTES

DATE	COMPANY	SERVICE/JOB	PRICE	THOUGHTS

PURCHASED BATHROOM 3 ITEMS

ITEM	SUPPLIER	COST
	TOTAL	

NOTES

_____
_____
_____
_____
_____
_____
_____
_____
_____
_____
_____
_____
_____
_____
_____
_____
_____
_____
_____
_____
_____

INTERIOR DESIGN PLAN

BATHROOM 4

DIMENSIONS _____

OF WINDOWS _____ # OF DOORS _____

WINDOW 1 SIZE _____ DOOR 1 _____

WINDOW 2 SIZE _____ DOOR 2 _____

WINDOW 3 SIZE _____ DOOR 3 _____

COLOR / STYLE _____

WALLS _____

FLOOR _____

CEILING _____

TRIM _____

DOORS _____

NOTES / IDEAS

BATHROOM 4 PLAN

BATHROOM 4 TO DO LIST

TASK	FINISHED

BATHROOM 4 QUOTES

DATE	COMPANY	SERVICE/JOB	PRICE	THOUGHTS

PURCHASED BATHROOM 4 ITEMS

ITEM	SUPPLIER	COST
	TOTAL	

NOTES

INTERIOR DESIGN PLAN
ENTRANCE / HALLWAY

DIMENSIONS _____

OF WINDOWS _____ # OF DOORS _____

WINDOW 1 SIZE _____ DOOR 1 _____

WINDOW 2 SIZE _____ DOOR 2 _____

WINDOW 3 SIZE _____ DOOR 3 _____

COLOR / STYLE _____

   WALLS _____

   FLOOR _____

   CEILING _____

   TRIM _____

   DOORS _____

NOTES / IDEAS

ENTRANCE / HALLWAY PLAN

ENTRANCE / HALLWAY TO DO LIST

TASK	FINISHED

ENTRANCE / HALLWAY QUOTES

DATE	COMPANY	SERVICE/JOB	PRICE	THOUGHTS

PURCHASED ENTRANCE / HALLWAY ITEMS

ITEM	SUPPLIER	COST
	TOTAL	

NOTES

DESIGN PLAN

GARDEN

DIMENSIONS _____

_____   _____

_____   _____

_____   _____

_____   _____

COLOR / STYLE _____

FENCE _____

GROUND _____

LIGHTING _____

SEATING _____

DECKING _____

NOTES / IDEAS

GARDEN PLAN

GARDEN TO DO LIST

TASK	FINISHED

GARDEN QUOTES

DATE	COMPANY	SERVICE/JOB	PRICE	THOUGHTS

PURCHASED GARDEN ITEMS

ITEM	SUPPLIER	COST
	TOTAL	

NOTES

INTERIOR DESIGN PLAN

_____

DIMENSIONS   _____

OF WINDOWS   _____   # OF DOORS   _____

WINDOW 1 SIZE   _____   DOOR 1   _____

WINDOW 2 SIZE   _____   DOOR 2   _____

WINDOW 3 SIZE   _____   DOOR 3   _____

COLOR / STYLE   _____

　　WALLS   _____

　　FLOOR   _____

　　CEILING   _____

　　TRIM   _____

　　DOORS   _____

NOTES / IDEAS

_____ PLAN

_____ TO DO LIST

TASK	FINISHED

_____ QUOTES

DATE	COMPANY	SERVICE/JOB	PRICE	THOUGHTS

PURCHASED _____ ITEMS

ITEM	SUPPLIER	COST
	TOTAL	

NOTES

INTERIOR DESIGN PLAN

_____

DIMENSIONS   _____

OF WINDOWS   _____   # OF DOORS   _____

WINDOW 1 SIZE   _____   DOOR 1   _____

WINDOW 2 SIZE   _____   DOOR 2   _____

WINDOW 3 SIZE   _____   DOOR 3   _____

COLOR / STYLE   _____

    WALLS   _____

    FLOOR   _____

    CEILING   _____

    TRIM   _____

    DOORS   _____

<u>NOTES / IDEAS</u>

PROJECT _____ PLAN

_____ TO DO LIST

TASK	FINISHED

_____ QUOTES

DATE	COMPANY	SERVICE/JOB	PRICE	THOUGHTS

PURCHASED _____ ITEMS

ITEM	SUPPLIER	COST
	TOTAL	

NOTES

INTERIOR DESIGN PLAN

_____

DIMENSIONS   _____

OF WINDOWS   _____   # OF DOORS   _____

WINDOW 1 SIZE   _____   DOOR 1   _____

WINDOW 2 SIZE   _____   DOOR 2   _____

WINDOW 3 SIZE   _____   DOOR 3   _____

COLOR / STYLE   _____

   WALLS   _____

   FLOOR   _____

   CEILING   _____

   TRIM   _____

   DOORS   _____

NOTES / IDEAS

_____ TO DO LIST

TASK	FINISHED

_____ QUOTES

DATE	COMPANY	SERVICE/JOB	PRICE	THOUGHTS

PURCHASED _____ ITEMS

ITEM	SUPPLIER	COST
	TOTAL	

NOTES

INTERIOR DESIGN PLAN

_____

DIMENSIONS   _____

OF WINDOWS   _____   # OF DOORS   _____

WINDOW 1 SIZE   _____   DOOR 1   _____

WINDOW 2 SIZE   _____   DOOR 2   _____

WINDOW 3 SIZE   _____   DOOR 3   _____

COLOR / STYLE   _____

   WALLS   _____

   FLOOR   _____

   CEILING   _____

   TRIM   _____

   DOORS   _____

NOTES / IDEAS

_____ PLAN

_____ TO DO LIST

TASK	FINISHED

_____ QUOTES

DATE	COMPANY	SERVICE/JOB	PRICE	THOUGHTS

PURCHASED _____ ITEMS

ITEM	SUPPLIER	COST
	TOTAL	

NOTES

NOTES

Made in the USA
Coppell, TX
06 August 2024

35624662R00070